This Book Belongs To:

____

BY
Home Planners And
Journals
To help you organize your life

SALAD

SALAD

SALAD

~ SALAD ~

~ SALAD ~